Writing Is The Happiness Of Sorrow

By the author

Prose
Twice is not enough
The Lake of Love
There Is Always Something More

Poetry
Palm Lines
The Beautiful Ones have been born
Light of Awakening
River
Cumbrian Lines: poems inspired by the Lake District

In Igbo
Mmiri a zoro nwayọ nwayọ

In German
Der Schlaf, aus dem ich wachend träume
Innengart
Das dauerhafte Gedicht

For Children:
Somayinozo's Stories

Che Chidi Chukwumerije – Writing Is The Happiness of Sorrow
Second Edition 2015.
First edition 2013 under the pseudonym Aka Teraka.
Boxwood Publishing House e.K.

Cover photo © Che Chidi Chukwumerije.

Che Chidi Chukwumerije

WRITING IS THE HAPPINESS OF SORROW

Poems

...

Boxwood Publishing House, Frankfurt

Table of contents

–

Dedicated to my late brother

Kwame Ekwueme Chukwumerije

who also discovered the
consoling power of writing
shortly before his departure

for you
nothing is enough
–

Writing Is The Happiness Of Sorrow

Writing is the happiness
Of sorrow
The immortal spirit
Of mortality
The voice that needs
No mouth
The painting whose canvas is
The reader's mind.

Hatred And Hope

Branded roses
Blood is your dance floor
Beast is the yeast of your flour
Your moist garden is the handle of my door
And your soup is dour.

I saw a stranger, dressed in black,
Quietly step back from your door –
I saw you, a black bird in grey skies
Flapping, rising
Hatred flaming in your chest like
A torn rose.

Yet I kissed you, don't
Ask me why – your lips parted and I tasted
Hope on your tongue
Like a squirrel hiding in the bush.

A Little Weird

You have to be a little weird
To be normal
A little fat to be healthy
A little perverted to love fully
A little poor to be rich
And a little me
To be you.

Waving Goodbye

When I started to interact with you
Little did I understand
That true friendship is an addiction
Too hurtful for lonely people

Metamorphosis from yesterday's amnesia
To today's cage of painful memories
Was like dawn that swiftly recedes
Unobserved.

The numbing melody of a thousand shards
Crashing to the splintered ground
Is a sad song
Yet I must dance alone.

Life has petalled pain
With the scent of a red rose
A caged rainbow beats in my chest
Like Harmattan waving goodbye to the rains.

The January Blues

They say it's grey
Sometimes white
Intuitions in the cradle
Of hazy light

When a feeling
Feels like a feeling
And a thought
Cannot be caught

And January does
What December should've
The plunge is depth
It is full of

Regret and hope
And Resolution
And birth and blues
And vision.

Once So Deep, Now So Shallow

Once so deep, now so shallow
Once never walking the path I now follow
My farm lies fallow

Another dimension
Same old sung in a new key
Sharps, naturals, empty flats
We've moved house, you, I

I like it that there is no barrier
In between
MY view into your eyes, your view into my heart –
It gives me hope
Furnishes me with counterproof more powerful
Than the deliberations of thoughts

Did you renounce anything for this love, this hour, this
Life? – The words grow stronger
The more I write; the light grows brighter
Within the night, beneath the descending Halo.

Accuracy Without Equal

Accuracy without equal
You, mystery, cut me, down, fusillade, hot bullets
Ripping, skin, flesh, meat, bones,
DisOrganing
Back, broken neck, shattered plastered skull
Punctured lungs, lifeless spasmodically jerking limbs
Unforgettable eyes, flaming heart
You reduced me to zero
Anew I build
The same old poem. Again.

World and nature touch off in me
Memory, understanding
Source of beginning

Accuracy without equal, you touched off
My very I.

Parting Fully

I should have gone home, shouldn't I?
Should not have bothered at all coming
It's all over.
Because of you I've walked in mud
Battled through thick forest
Trudged in rain, cold, sneezing
Borne questioning look after looking question
I had no answers
Borne and missed all my goals
Seeking yours
Aye, I should have gone home, shouldn't I?
Should not have bothered coming to you at all –
Yet it's good I did
For we must thoroughly experience the End
In order to be grateful to be free of one another
For good.

The End Must Be Strong

The end must be strong
Or it will not be satisfied with itself
Shall return again
Again
Demanding to be ended...

The end that drags out must be allowed to drag out
That way we shall never forget
It is imprinted, chiselled, branded prime-deeply
Into heart and mind
Unforgettable, memorable, forever recognisable
Never to be dared again.

Closing Doors

The doors shut, swiftly and sure
They open again and again they close
Gradually, gradually speed gives way to slowness
The doors close swiftly
Remain shut
All over.

Depths

Now we think before we talk
And talk about our thoughts
But never about the cause of our thoughts
I used to think that thoughts were what?
If the fan rotates, the air will swirl
Powerful draft
When the heart surges, mind turns
Words emerge.

Sealing Up

Silent things, unnamed
Unnameable, nameless
Lie between us like yesterday

Why does yesterday
Continue always to exist?
Why doesn't it just go away forever?

Why must we understand yesterday
In order to understand today?
Why do we even bother to seek for
Understanding amongst our human selves?
Mystery
The very mystery itself, no answer

Round and round. I can't bear it
When we fight, dear.

Yes, Friends Also Say Goodbye Sometimes

The lash of the whipping of the bird's wings
The pitch of the whistling of the bird, it sings
The moan of the memory of all those things
That went wrong in the life of all those kings
That ruled the lives of men.

Outward appearances all over, all over, all over
Who can completely and truly know the other?
Look deeper, look further, look beneath the cover
Kings are but people too, my wife, her lover, I discover
Was not one, they were ten.

I pick up my pen and I write you a letter
As you read it, your eyes get wet, then wetter
Yet despite, or because of, tears we do now feel better
Looking into each other's eyes through this piercingly open letter
Letterspace in exchange for a den.

Bird is joyously asking me from beside my heart
Can I be allowed to become your extra part?
Why sure! Right away it does start
To write its way into my heart
Dear, you'll now need a new chart
If you wish to read me with any ken
And that's one zen
You can't purchase with yen
But maybe can repossess with the right stroke of thy pen
If you have the courage to try...

A soft sound, a gently cry
The opportunity just passed us by...
Goodbye.

Writing Nightly

I cannot stop writing
But, I won't lie, I sometimes try to
But I was a poet long before I was born
And when I write it freely and simply I am shorn
Anew, like sheep, my wool will grow again
And again poetry will shave me of my pain
And it is at night, when everything is calm
That, writing, I feel most at home.

My Poetry Bench

There is a graveyard thence
With benches placed all over
Where people come a-steady
To ponder life and death

There is a certain bench
Apart from every other
Where I sit when poetry
Takes clean away my breath.

Jazz Hole

I'm feeling down today
The perfect mood
For poetry

He's played the music
So long
He's lost in the music now

That musician on stage
Is an echo of the poetry
Eating me inside.

Hurt

When will he stop
Persecuting that guitar
His voice is hoarse
It hurts me

It digs a hole in my armour
Roughly
And scoops me out
Hoarsely

I wish I could remember him
In my dream tonight
When silence is wall
Enclosing me, she's gone

His voice is gruff
A street musician
Enjoying his moment on stage
Roughly.

The Happy Sadness Of Musicians

Every Tuesday
They gather here
A flock of wild geese
And play for nobody

Their smiles
Each time their smiles
Break my heart
Open stage

Not a dime
What's their crime?
Listen in
To the sound of happiness

It is full of sadness
Life is music
Friends are memory
Death is immortality.

Amnesia

It's so easy to forget
Who you are
The longer you live like them
With them
Amongst them

Sleep is depth
Is debt
Is death

The greatest treasure on earth
Is memory

It's so easy to forget
Who you are
On earth.
Everything seems normal
To sleepwalker.

Joker

Jokes are the barrier
People let down between themselves
A spoken word can wash away years of building
Leave in its wake a ruptured earth
Worse than as if life never happened.

Watch that joke, it's no joke
The damage will outlive the laughter
Long long after
The careless word you spoke.

The Work Day

The work day
Goes its work way
Grows old on youth

A bitter way to learn the truth
The pita pata of small talk
Walks up and down the corridor

The emerging thunder
The beginning
Hold on, strong.

Quick And Painful

The pain
Of gainlessness
Stainless steel
Grooveless will
Mad dash through the day
Quick and painful get it over with
Madness is a mask
Undon it – when the soft breeze
Of evening awakens, soothingly, quiet perception again
At home again
The painlessness
Of gain. When the chapter
Has been closed. It was worth it.

Discerning

I fear
The daily commute
To the valley of the mute
The echoless cry of my silent flute
Digs a hole in my soul
Wringe me mad
I fear

Mockery sticks his head around the door
You no waving yo flag no mo?
Blackhawk down
My dreams, stranded shipwrecks
Scuttle each hurriedly into safety
Hiding they fearfully await the scorching passage
Of the locals' raging raid –
Some will be caught, shot, mocked
Some will sacrifice themselves
That the finer ones may escape the drape
For tomorrow's blossoming

Quiet now
Wait for the Sign.

Daily Trainride Into Materialism

In the skyline gray
My memory hung
Future had gone astray
This emptiness stung
Hung with reality in the greying city
Dying trees, loveless pity
Duplicity and winding and twisting, reflecting
The beast in the best of the robots erecting
Their concrete phalli, their bull's I's, to scratch the sky
Insatiable itch, impotent ambition, try and try
And try as you might, your might is the limp cloud
The wilted grass, the lonely office, the empty crowd
The quiet madness, the gory glory
The daily trainride into another same story
The casual business of getting by
Between yesterday and tomorrow
A moment of reflection, gone, a sigh
Of something neither joy nor remorse.

Setting Moon

The city is overcast with the blue mist of dawn
Swiftly fading
The street lamps of night
Hurriedly dwindling
Yesterday's man
Softly gazing
A tiger's cub at the setting moon.

Beauty Unseen

I'm moving through my destiny
Like a train at night
So much beauty in the world out there
But I race past it all
Looking out the window
I see mostly myself
And when I look through myself
Sometimes, dimly
The light of distant houses
And vague patches of field and snow.

Ghosts In The Train Station

The snow at night
It's coming to me
Like a circle of friends
Ghosts around I feel them
Quiet like the snow

What do you want?
Hanging around at the train station
Accompanying the living
Silently
As they come and go...
Pack your bags and go too
Board the train and ride on home.

Meet Me At The Terminal

It's been a while since I took the train
Down memory lane
The canvas was painted on the rain
Pictures of joy and pain

A tree is bent in the wind
The wind is bent on blowing
A tunnel light went through my mind
And time has gone a-borrowing

A path is snaking through the fields
I'm meandering through my thoughts
A bird is flying over me
It is my intuition, caught

And then I remember my childhood friend
My brother, full of life
His train met an untimely end
His smile keeps me alive

When my trainride starts to wear me down
This silent speeding through the grey
His sun comes through, memory's crown
His smile reminds me of the way

Paradise, he decided, was his goal
Self-communion became
The watchful escort of his soul
The transfiguration the same

The weight of suffering is made light
By kindness and bravery
Let humour sometimes mask your insight
And silence our story.

What you saw at the beginning
Is what you'll see at the end
Through life's tunnels, guard safely within
Our hard-won Faith, brotherfriend

Memory, rested in peace
Grows pregnant with time
Comes full circle as distance recedes
Equally crossed by thine and mine.

A face fades in the window
Breath or fog adieu?
Swing chariot, swing low
I will be waiting for you.

Back on track, the humming, the ride
My life flashes past like a countryside
Destination is a few minutes away
A thousand years are just another day
The borrowed time, who will repay?
The price is pride.

The iron rails, impersonal
Bound to ride out, like a criminal
This cycle carnal –
Friend of my youth, youth eternal
Meet me at the terminal.

For Kwame (30.4.75 – 6.4.95)
I will never betray.

Full Moons

The moons turned around
Showed me their backs
I was surprised to see
Their faces not their backs
Staring back at me.

She who I thought was my friend
Stabbed me in the back
Wrapped the wool around my wound
I could not see
What I could feel
The cold sacrificial fire burning
Beneath my trust.

He who I believed to be my detractor
Was always my protector, in retrospect
Has become my dearest instructor
I never said thank you for shrugging
And understanding me.

Bird Soul

We plan for tomorrow
Unsure
Of whether we will meet it –
This is the joy of life
The moment.

Today's joy
Is the conquest of tomorrow's sorrow
Today's life the defeat
Of tomorrow's death
Plan for tomorrow
And be happy today.

The future cannot take the moment
Away from you.

Sportsman's Ship

Sports is war
Defeat is death
Victory is life
The spirit draws its lesson
As quietly its days lessen
And it draws its last breath.

Draw your straw
Face your draw
Everybody has a lesson to draw
From the draw
Thus ends every victory and defeat in a Draw
Claw your way out
Of the truncheon of doubt
Learn what the bout
Is really about.

It's about you!
Finding you!
Experiencing you!
Conquering you!
Knowing you!
Loving you!
Becoming you!
It's about you!

Sports is war
With yourself –
When you've found your answer
Ignore the music of the record books
Book your ticket on the ship of life
Sail on sunny day...

Dramatic Duel

A duel
Is an exchange
Of energies

Synergies rule

A duel
Is a clash
Of ideologies

Mentalities

Nadal vs Federer
Djokovic vs Nadal
Barcelona vs Real
Nigeria vs Cameroon
You think it's happening at top speed
Look again: it's in slow motion
First it happened inside
Then it slowly squeezes itself out
Never mind the drama

Thirsty

I loved many women
But none stilled my thirst
Then I loved my thirst
And I was stilled.

Pick With Care
The Enemies Your Bear

Pick with care
The enemies you bear
When the unexpected is near
They shall be there
To crown you.

When true friends
Step off the boat
Curious, how the river
Turns your coat
Around you.

Clear your throat
Vomit when no-one is looking
Regurgitated oaths
Pressure-cooking
Sunbrowns you.

If diplomacy
Be their tactless god
How shall he decipher
Your non-committal nod,
Proud you?

But brave soldier
It is the art of war
To live on in pages
Of folklore
Unbound to you.

Art In All Its Forms

Art in all its forms
Is the thief of time
Stealing from the past
Sharing with the present
And the future
Like Robin Hood
For time is wealthy in memory
And, like Shylock, reluctant to give.

An evening song will reawaken your life's morning
A painting will view like déjà vu from lives unremembered
And a poem will whisper your life's story back to you.

The True Brotherhood Is In The Heart

Brotherhood
Inner understanding
If missing
All the blood in the world
Won't bridge it.

Gaps remain
Where cracks cause pain.

Spirit

Crash
The gates of brain
Break into
Realm of soul

Deep within ethereal expanse
See a mountain of fire
Sanctuary
Of spirit

Spirit is flame
Warms and illumines
Soul

Brain is mirror
Reflects only when
Wiped clean

Through the damaged river
Darkly

We grope.

Loneliness

Loneliness comes in little sips
Quiet mornings in maddening intervals
Herald recognition
Larger and larger swathes of universe
Dying into blackhole.

The louder we laugh
The less we can bear the sound
Of silence
Only the lonely heart is left in the end
The quietness of Now.

River, River, Flowing Home

I saw a departed soul
There
On the other side of the river
Yet there as no bridge
Across the river
How did he get there?
How did he cross to the other
Side of the river?

River, river, flowing home
River, river, flowing home

Bathed in the mild glows of
The fields across
The river
Stood a soul
And he said, brother
Goodbye

River, river, flowing home
River, river, flowing, flowing home...

The Pure Flower

Everywhere I sought it
I sought in every land
To know if Nature'd wrought it
Anywhere 'neath her hand
But though I searched with all my might
And though I looked forever
I've never seen before my sight
An ugly flower ever.

Although she's rare to see
Or on the earth be seen
Through land or on the sea
As though she ne'er hath been
Yet when ever this Flower blossoms
When this Flower blooms
Pure beauty's all I see in dozens
In all my heart's rooms.

Did Heaven ever come to earth?
Did Beauty ever give birth?
The pure woman is Heaven's flower
Heaven's beauty, Heaven's grace and Heaven's power.

Smiles

She had so many smiles inside her heart
And at every opportunity that came her way
She would release one of them
Readily, happily, she would gladly part
With a smile for any one or thing day after day
And each smile of hers was a gem

Though sorrow and heartache would often cross her path
Though hatred and evil would often be her lot
Yet she never ever failed to smile
A smile from the heart was her substitute for wrath
A quiet cool smile for when things got hot
As precious as the ancient Nile

The years went by and she grew very old
But her innate warmth refused to grow any cold
And she continued to smile
And anybody who was burdened with cares untold
And anybody on whom sorrow had a hold
Was refreshed by her smile

To smile and smile and never run out of smiles
To give and give and never desist from giving
From the stat to the end
She smiles, she smiles, forevermore she smiles
And though she's now dead, she's definitely still living
Smiling even past the end.

My Heart

A broken heart, how shall it mend?
Who shall this garden tend?
My heart, my heart, break not, nor bend
But remain ever into every end
My unwavering friend.

Always There

I saw three things up in the sky
Two birds and the moon
The birds flew away
While the moon remained
For a few hours,
And then was also gone...

Will you make me a promise, love
Never to be gone?
But like the sky be always there
Even when all else is gone.

Blessed Be They
Who Work In The Field

A smile, a wave, from where did it come?
From beyond the earth, or heaven, or where?
We feel it, we see it, reflect it here from
And spread it the earth round, here there, everywhere

Blessed be they who work in the field
Who work with their hands in the soil
Blessed be they who, yield after yield
And season on season yet toil.

The end, the start, the middle of work
Like fishers at sea, unceasing, we roll
Like all true handworkers who never ever shrink
The call and the urging perceived in the soul

Blessed be they who work in the field
Who link man and nature on earth
Blessed be they, in them doth life shield
The true future waiting for birth.

Girl I Love You

Girl I love you
Yes I do
Love will us do
Through and through

Is the sky blue?
Are we two?
We are one true
Heartbeat too

Please be simple
Evermore
Please be simple
Evermore

The First Thing

What you first saw is what you'll see last
What you first met and left
Waits in the future, not in the past –
Of them is man never bereft.

Flow, flow, go, go
Reap now what once you did sow
Flow, flow, sow, sow
What you would reap tomorrow.

Friends that we first knew, friends that we loved
Friends that we lost and forgot
Come back to claim us with love undissolved –
Did it die? Oh, no, it did not.

The temple, the heart, the present, the past
The questions, the answers, the path
Humility first, humility last
Serving the Light in which we bath.

Wait Upon Ours

Wait upon me
You who woke me first
You made me thirsty
Now come quench this thirst

Today is all we all we all we have
Not yesterday, not tomorrow
Today today is all we have
To follow.

We Are Friends

Not because of what you did
Or did not do
Not because of what you said
Or failed to say
Not because of what you know
Or never came to know

But because in your eyes I espy
A certain thing
Which I cannot immediately define
But by which I have hope
That you will be the important one in my life...

Patience.

Your Eyes

Who will it be
After me?
Who will it be
Baby?

Who could make it
Like it was?
Who could take it
And leave no flaws?

Never forget me
Little tease
Never forget me
Please.

Shiver

The quiet quiet of that night over there
Look, that night is waiting over there
What a night! Quiet and black
The blackness swallowing up the fullmoon
It is a blind night
With a will so dark it smothers
It's starry children
And blinds its one bright eye.

I shiver
As you approach
I shiver
As you reach out to me
I shiver
As you approach
Baby, I shiver.

I hesitate to look out through the window
Into the distance
At that night waiting for me
Me and my heart, my sojourning heart

The eerie cat is silent with fear
The snake slithers hastily away
I fear that night, but I must approach it
With my heart of flames – I am the sun
The cold sun.

The Inability To Break

As hard as hardness was
As steady as the flickering flame
As rough as the tree-bark
So was the Song

The mighty flow of the river
Magnified in the crashing of the Sea
The living Sea

The simple Morningsong of the bird
Will outsing this Song so strong
And will move hearts
With a power more elemental
Than the river and the Sea.

So So

Say it so – so so
Do it so – so so

Vulgar reality
Cover it up diplomatically
Virtual reality

So! So!

Propensity

The roots are deep
Deeper than the vows we keep
When we sleep
The roots are deep
Of the many fruits we tend to reap.

The road is steep
The road that leads into the deep
Where we keep
The tears we weep
In the grip of propensity deep.

Old-Fashioned Values

If you give your word, keep it too
Maybe it's just an old-fashioned virtue
But it makes others respect you
And you'll feel good too
And it breeds harmony between me and you

Oh, I think these new times
Are in need of some old-fashioned values
An intuitive heart will grasp them
An over-intellectual mind will narrow them
Because they're old old old-fashioned values

Honour is more than a word
It's the character you wear, the cross you bear
The thoughts you think and words you say
It's the nature of your intuitive perception
It's your readiness to stand by your Intuition
Even when you can't yet quite put it in words

There's a certain purity somewhere in the heart of honour
Maybe it's just an old-fashioned virtue
But it makes others respect you
And you'll feel right too
And it breeds harmony between others and you

Oh I think the new times coming
Are in need of some old-fashioned values
An intuitive heart will grasp them
But an over-intellectual mind will narrow them
Because they're old old old-fashioned values.

Sellers On The Street

Driver, why are you so irritated
By the seller at your window?
It's easy to judge
Easy to hiss and insult
But think a little, think a little

What do you think it was
That drove him out of his house
And unto the street
To stand there through sun and rain
Day after day – selling any little thing

Was it mindlessness at the comfort of others
Or the struggle for existence?

Writing Is The Happiness Of Sorrow